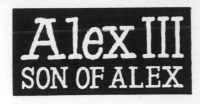

Alex III
SON OF ALEX

Alex III
SON OF ALEX

PENGUIN BOOKS

PENGUIN BOOKS

Published by the Penguin Group
Penguin Books Ltd, 27 Wrights Lane, London W8 5TZ, England
Viking Penguin, a division of Penguin Books USA Inc.
375 Hudson Street, New York, New York 10014, USA
Penguin Books Australia Ltd, Ringwood, Victoria, Australia
Penguin Books Canada Ltd, 2801 John Street, Markham, Ontario, Canada L3R 1B4
Penguin Books (NZ) Ltd, 182–190 Wairau Road, Auckland 10, New Zealand

Penguin Books Ltd, Registered Offices: Harmondsworth, Middlesex England

These cartoon strips first appeared in the *Independent*
Published in Penguin Books 1990
1 3 5 7 9 10 8 6 4 2

Additional material by Mark Warren

The moral right of the authors has been asserted

Printed in England by Clays Ltd, St Ives plc

Penny
(Alex's wife.)

Rupert
(Alex's boss.)

Greg.
(Alex's brother,
a journalist.)

Alex

Clive

Ruth
(American trader.)

Bridget
(Clive's girlfriend.)

Vince
(a money broker)

Alex
PEATTIE + TAYLOR

I THINK I'M LOOKING FORWARD TO THIS CORPORATE HOSPITALITY CRICKET WEEKEND AS MUCH AS THE CLIENTS.

SAME HERE.

IT'S NOT EVERY DAY ONE GETS THE CHANCE TO PLAY AGAINST A TEAM OF CRICKETING CELEBRITIES IN THE ELEGANT GROUNDS OF AN ENGLISH STATELY HOME.

ABSOLUTELY.

JUST IMAGINE IT: A PLEASANT DRIVE DOWN IN THE MORNING... A DECENT LUNCH AND AFTERWARDS A CHANCE TO FULFILL ONE'S SCHOOLBOY AMBITION OF CATCHING OUT IAN BOTHAM.

ACTUALLY, IAN, THE PORT GETS PASSED TO THE LEFT.

WIDE.

Alex
PEATTIE + TAYLOR

GOODNESS. WHAT A JOURNEY IN... THAT'S THE LAST TIME I ACCEPT A LIFT IN ALEX'S CAR.

DO YOU KNOW WE WERE STUCK IN A TRAFFIC JAM FOR AN HOUR AND A HALF...

OH NO... AND IT'S SWELTERING HOT TODAY.

IT MUST HAVE BEEN UNCOMFORTABLE.

IT WAS... AND ALEX REFUSED TO LET ME OPEN A WINDOW...

LOOK, CLIVE, THIS IS ONE OF THE FEW DAYS IN THE YEAR WHEN OTHER ROAD-USERS ARE ABLE TO FULLY APPRECIATE THE EFFECTIVENESS OF MY CAR'S AIR-CONDITIONING SYSTEM.

I HAD GOOSEFLESH ALL OVER.

Alex
PEATTIE + TAYLOR

LISTEN TO THIS: "IT HAS BEEN FOUND THAT MYSTIFYING NERVE PAINS IN THE UPPER THIGH WHICH AFFLICT CERTAIN YOUNG MALE PATIENTS..."

"ARE CAUSED BY SPENDING LONG HOURS SITTING AT A DESK OR IN CARS WITH A BACK POCKET TOO FULL OF HARD PLASTIC CREDIT CARDS WHICH PRESS AGAINST THE BUTTOCK".

"DOCTORS SAY THAT THIS DISCOVERY NOW MAKES IT OBVIOUS HOW TO TREAT THESE PATIENTS."

PRIVATELY.

THAT'S RIGHT... A FULL COURSE OF CONSULTATIONS... EXTENSIVE TESTS... VISITS TO SPECIALISTS...

Alex
PEATTIE + TAYLOR

RUTH, YOU'RE AMERICAN... DO YOU KNOW ANYTHING ABOUT THESE SO-CALLED "BOUDOIR PHOTOGRAPHS"?

SURE.

LIKE WHEN HIGHLY PAID FEMALE EXECUTIVES WHO, FOR EXAMPLE WORK IN A BANK AND WHOSE PUBLIC PERSONA IS DICTATED BY THE WORKPLACE, DRESS UP IN PROVOCATIVE CLOTHES TO BE PHOTOGRAPHED IN PRIVATE PORTRAIT STUDIOS?

ER... YES...

IT'S VERY POPULAR IN THE STATES. I'VE DONE IT MYSELF. IT'S A CHANCE TO BRING OUT A DIFFERENT IMAGE OF YOURSELF AS A WOMAN BESIDES THAT OF THE STRAIGHT-LACED WORKING GIRL.

OH... ER...

LOOK, HERE'S ONE OF ME WEARING TROUSERS.

STEADY ON...

THEY'RE CALVIN KLEIN, BUSTER.

Alex
PEATTIE + TAYLOR

THAT'S RATHER A GENEROUS DONATION TO YOUR OLD COLLEGE.

WELL, WHEN I GOT THE LETTER FROM THE UNIVERSITY TO ALL ITS GRADUATES ASKING FOR CONTRIBUTIONS...

CAMPAIGN FOR OXFORD

I LOOKED AT THE EXAMPLE OF MY GRANDFATHER, WHO AS A SUCCESSFUL BUSINESSMAN HAS NEVER FAILED TO LEND HIS FINANCIAL SUPPORT TO EDUCATIONAL CHARITIES...

CAMPAIGN FOR OXFORD

BECAUSE HE'S ALWAYS REGRETTED THAT LACK OF MONEY PREVENTED HIM FROM HAVING THE OPPORTUNITY OF A DECENT EDUCATION HIMSELF... SO MAKING THIS DONATION GIVES ME A GOOD FEELING...

CAMPAIGN FOR OXFORD

KNOWING THAT THIS IS ONE APPEAL HE COULD NEVER BE INVITED TO CONTRIBUTE TO.

CAMPAIGN FOR OXFORD

Alex PEATTIE + TAYLOR

ALEX GREW UP LOVING ALL THOSE HOLLYWOOD BLACK AND WHITE FILMS FROM THE FORTIES.

BUT WHEN HE WAS IN THE STATES HE SAW ONE OF THOSE NEW ARTIFICIALLY COLOURED PRINTS OF 'CASABLANCA' ON VIDEO.

HE WAS ABSOLUTELY HORRIFIED BY WHAT THEY'D DONE.

WAS THE FILM TOTALLY RUINED FOR HIM?

WELL, FINDING OUT AFTER ALL THESE YEARS THAT HUMPHREY BOGART WORE A BROWN SUIT WAS A PRETTY TRAUMATIC EXPERIENCE.

Alex PEATTIE + TAYLOR

EUR! THIS HORRID LITTLE JAPANESE GADGET MAKES THE SOUND OF A LOO FLUSHING.

FWSHHH

YES. JAPANESE LADIES CARRY THEM.

WHATEVER FOR?

WELL, IN THIN-WALLED JAPANESE HOUSES ACUTE SOCIAL EMBARRASSMENT CAN BE AVOIDED...

IF GUESTS USE THESE WHILE GOING TO THE LOO TO COVER THE SOUND OF THEIR ABLUTIONS.

WELL I DON'T KNOW WHY YOU'RE TAKING IT TO CLIVE'S GARDEN PARTY.

FWWSHHH

COME OUT OF THERE, ALEX.

LOOK... IT REALLY IS A POTTING SHED ...HONESTLY...

Alex PEATTIE + TAYLOR

THIS ALL FEELS SO WRONG, RUTH. I'M NOT SURE I CAN JUST GET CALMLY INTO YOUR BED LIKE THIS.

WHAT'S THE PROBLEM, CLIVE?

WELL, MAYBE IF YOU TRIED DRESSING UP A BIT.. PUT ON SOME SUSPENDERS...

YOU'RE AMERICAN... NOT LIKE THE ENGLISH GIRLS... YOU UNDERSTAND WHAT I'M TALKING ABOUT...

SUSPENDERS HUH? SURE, CLIVE.

CLIVE, GET YOUR GODDAM BUTT INTO THAT BED.

YES, SIR.

Alex PEATTIE + TAYLOR

OH LOOK. CLIVE'S FOUND SOMEONE TO TALK TO ABOUT HIS FAVOURITE SUBJECT :- THE SHORTCOMINGS OF MODERN ARCHITECTURE.

PRINCE CHARLES!

FROM THE WAY H.R.H. IS TALKING IT'S QUITE HARD TO KNOW WHAT HIS OPINION OF POST-MODERNISM ACTUALLY IS.

I SUPPOSE HE HAS TO BE CAREFUL WHAT HE SAYS..

BUT I RECKON HE MUST HATE THOSE HIDEOUS IMPERSONAL CONSTRUCTIONS.

YES.

ONE MUST SOMETIMES WISH ONE COULD LEND ONE'S WEIGHT TO THE DISCUSSION.

PERHAPS ONE MIGHT BE TEMPTED TO AGREE WITH ONE...

..BUT ETIQUETTE PROHIBITS THE USE OF 1ST AND 2ND PERSON PRONOUNS.

Alex PEATTIE + TAYLOR

THE PRESS PORTRAY ME AS SOME SORT OF FREAK BUT I SEE MYSELF AS A NORMAL BLOKE.

AND I LIKE TO THINK THAT PEOPLE IN THE STREET RELATE TO ME AND HEED MY OPINIONS...

MAYBE I'M FLATTERING MYSELF BUT I BELIEVE I HAVE THE EAR OF THE COMMON MAN.

WELL...DO YOU THINK I DO?

ER..

AT LEAST HIS DON'T GO THIS PECULIAR COLOUR, CLIVE.

Alex PEATTIE + TAYLOR

I HEAR YOU TOOK A PHOTOGRAPH WHEN THAT GIRL STREAKED AT THE TEST MATCH THE OTHER DAY.

GOT IT HERE. SHE WAS SITTING RIGHT BESIDE ME.

CARUTHERS BROUGHT HER ALONG FOR THE DAY... ONE MINUTE WE WERE ALL WATCHING THE CRICKET...

MY WORD!

NEXT THING I KNEW, SHE'D THROWN ALL HER CLOTHES ON THE SEAT AND WAS RACING OFF ACROSS THE PITCH STARK NAKED.

POOR CARUTHERS. HE MUST BE SO EMBARRASSED.

YES.

NOT EXACTLY JANET REGER IS IT?

WHAT A REVELATION.

Alex PEATTIE + TAYLOR

FOR ME, ONE OF THE BIGGEST PERKS ABOUT WORKING IN THE CITY IS BEING INVITED TO WIMBLEDON EACH YEAR AND GETTING TO MEET ALL THE TOP PLAYERS.

FASCINATING PEOPLE... THEIR EARNINGS ARE QUITE COLOSSAL, YOU KNOW... AND SOME OF THEM ARE AMAZINGLY YOUNG AS WELL.

ACCORDING TO THEM WIMBLEDON IS STILL THE TOPS, BUT IT'S PRETTY GRUELLING WHEN YOU'RE ON THE CIRCUIT YEAR AFTER YEAR.

I CAN WELL IMAGINE...

ASCOT, HENLEY, LE MANS... LORDS... IT MUST LEAVE EVEN THE MOST DYNAMIC EXECUTIVE QUITE EXHAUSTED.

I SAY. ISN'T THAT SIR GORDON GRAVES, THE CHIEF EXECUTIVE OF METROBANK? ...OVER THERE, BEHIND BORIS BECKER...

Alex PEATTIE+TAYLOR

BAD NEWS, PENNY. THE COMPANY WE'RE REPRESENTING IN THIS TAKEOVER HAS CALLED A MEETING FOR NEXT MONDAY.

OF COURSE IF ALL CONTINUES TO GO TO PLAN THAT'S LIKELY TO BE THE DAY YOU GIVE BIRTH...

WHAT ARE YOU GOING TO DO?

WELL, I'M ON PRETTY GOOD TERMS WITH THE M.D. I THOUGHT I MIGHT HAVE A WORD WITH HIM IN PRIVATE... ASK IF THERE ISN'T SOME WAY IT COULD BE PUT BACK OR BROUGHT FORWARD A DAY OR TWO...

WELL, I SUPPOSE YOU COULD ALWAYS HAVE AN INDUCED BIRTH, ALEX.

R.J. PHIBBS M.D.

GOOD IDEA, DOC. MAYBE WE COULD LEAVE A RUSK DOWN AT THE END OF THE BED...

Alex PEATTIE+TAYLOR

THIS IS TYPICAL OF MY LUCK. WE'RE SUPPOSED TO BE HAVING A SECRET AFFAIR AND YOUR FAN BELT SNAPS IN THE MIDDLE OF PICCADILLY CIRCUS.

I'M GOING TO NEED ONE OF YOUR STOCKINGS.

DON'T WORRY, CLIVE. THE A.A. WILL BE HERE SOON.

THEY'LL BE AGES. GIVE ME THE STOCKING.

IF YOU'RE SURE YOU KNOW WHAT YOU'RE DOING...

THIS IS ANOTHER FINE MESH YOU'VE GOT ME INTO...

Alex
PEATTIE + TAYLOR

WHAT'S HAPPENED, ALEX?

I'VE JUST HEARD PENNY'S GONE INTO LABOUR... AND I'M STUCK OUT HERE IN FRANKFURT.

I'M DESPERATE TO BE PRESENT AT THE BIRTH BUT ALL THE SCHEDULED FLIGHTS ARE FULLY BOOKED... SO I'VE CHARTERED A PLANE.

I'M WAITING TO HEAR BACK FROM THEM NOW.

RING

AH...

HELLO?....OH.... A FALSE ALARM YOU SAY?...HOW DISAPPOINTING...IS PENNY COMFORTABLE?

WELL AS COMFORTABLE AS CAN BE EXPECTED IN AN ARRIVALS HALL...

FRANKFURT FLUGHAFEN
←Ausgang, Exit.

GOOD, PUT HER ON THE NEXT FLIGHT BACK WOULD YOU?

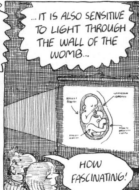

Alex PEATTIE + TAYLOR

I'VE BEEN READING ABOUT TECHNIQUES OF CHILDBIRTH IN PRIMITIVE TRIBES... IT MAKES ONE QUESTION A LOT OF THE PROCEDURES CONSIDERED STANDARD IN THIS DAY AND AGE.

WHEN I SEE PENNY, LYING HERE SURROUNDED BY HIGHLY-PAID SPECIALISTS AND A VERITABLE BATTERIE OF UP-TO-THE-MINUTE TECHNOLOGY...

I WONDER IF PERHAPS WE SHOULDN'T BE LEARNING A LESSON FROM SOME OF THESE ANCIENT PEOPLES.

ARE YOU ON ABOUT RED INDIANS AGAIN, ALEX?

I'VE TOLD YOU, I AM NOT HAVING MY BABY CALLED "BUPA OBSTETRICIAN" OR "PRIVATE BIRTHING ROOM".

NAMING THE BABY AFTER THE FIRST THING THE MOTHER SEES AFTER THE BIRTH SEEMS RATHER A GOOD IDEA TO ME.

Alex PEATTIE + TAYLOR

THIS IS DREADFUL.

OH OH OH.

THERE MUST BE SOMETHING THAT CAN BE DONE TO STOP THE PAIN.

GNGH...

I KNOW WHAT MIGHT HELP...

OH OH OH...

SORRY, PENNY, BUT THEY WERE REALLY DIGGING INTO MY HAND.

CLIP.

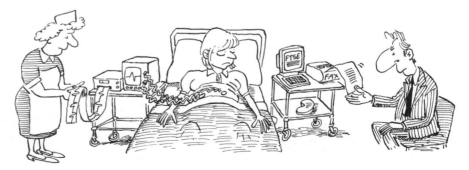

Alex PEATTIE + TAYLOR

WE'RE JUST GOING TO TAKE YOUR BABY OFF AND WEIGH HIM NOW...

BUT DON'T WORRY... BEFORE HE LEAVES THE ROOM WE ATTACH THESE LITTLE TAGS TO HIS WRISTS AND ANKLES...

WHAT A GOOD IDEA.

NOW THERE'S A SERVICE YOU DON'T GET ON THE N.H.S., PENNY..

ACTUALLY ALL NEWBORN BABIES ARE GIVEN THESE LABELS.

BUT N.H.S. BABIES DON'T COST ANYTHING.

ALEX, THEY'RE NAME TAGS.

Alex PEATTIE + TAYLOR

I DON'T KNOW WHAT DOCTORS CALL IT... "NIPPLE REFLEX" OR SOMETHING...

BUT AS SOON AS THE BABY IS BORN THERE'S THIS AMAZING INSTINCT TO SUCK.

IS THAT SO?

TAKE IT FROM ME, CLIVE. IT'S SOMETHING BASIC-AND I THINK PEOPLE SHOULD REMEMBER THAT... I'M ALL FOR IT.

WHAT, IN PUBLIC?

WHY NOT?.. I KNOW SOME PEOPLE ARE EMBARRASSED BY THE SEXUAL CONNOTATIONS...

BUT IF YOU ASK ME THE BEST THING TO DO IS IGNORE EVERYONE ELSE AND JUST WOP OUT THE OLD... - YOU KNOW...

CIGARS?

PRECISELY. BIG FAT ONES.

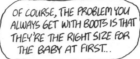

Alex PEATTIE + TAYLOR

WHAT'S THAT, ALEX?

VOICE-RESPONSE ALARM CLOCK.

THE ALARM SOUNDS, YOU SHOUT AT IT AND IT SWITCHES ITSELF OFF... THEN, IF NOT SWITCHED OFF MANUALLY, THE ALARM SOUNDS AGAIN AFTER 3 MINUTES AND SO ON...

LET'S TEST IT OUT.

ZZZ

BEEEP! BEEEP! BEEEP!

WAAAH!

BEEE...

EXCELLENT. IT WORKS.

THIS'LL TEACH HIM TO KEEP US AWAKE ALL NIGHT.

ZZZ

Alex PEATTIE + TAYLOR

I HEAR YOU'VE LET THREE MORE ANALYSTS GO, RUPERT.

YES, IT SEEMS WE'RE HAVING TO LET OUR WHOLE MARKET MAKING CAPACITY RUN DOWN QUIETLY.

RATHER A SHAME BUT, LIKE A LOT OF OTHER BANKS, WE'RE BEING FORCED TO PULL IN OUR HORNS AT THE MOMENT...

AND FRANKLY WE PROBABLY WENT INTO IT RATHER INDISCRIMINATELY IN THE FIRST PLACE AND NOW THE BANK CAN NO LONGER AFFORD THE LEVELS OF ACTIVITY WE ENJOYED IN THE OLD DAYS...

I SUPPOSE IT WOULD CREATE BAD PUBLICITY.

...SACKING 100 ALL IN ONE GO... IT WAS SUCH FUN, ALEX...

Alex PEATTIE+TAYLOR

I DON'T BELIEVE IT, RUTH! YOU'RE HAVING AN AFFAIR WITH CLIVE FROM CORPORATE FINANCE? HOW HAVE YOU KEPT IT A SECRET?

OH, YOU KNOW: DINNER DATES AT DARKENED TABLES AT THE BACK OF RARELY-FREQUENTED RESTAURANTS. SLIPPING BACK TO MY APARTMENT UNDER COVER OF DARKNESS...

BUT HE'S GOT A GIRLFRIEND. WHY'S HE DOING THIS?

OH, THE USUAL STORY. BOREDOM WITH HIS HIGHLY-PAID LIFESTYLE...

HE FEELS HE'S JUST GOING THROUGH THE MOTIONS OF WHAT'S EXPECTED OF HIM. HE SAYS IT'S ONLY WITH ME THAT HE CAN REALLY BE HIMSELF...

...TIMID, ANONYMOUS, FURTIVE, TOTALLY NON-OSTENTATIOUS...

I DON'T KNOW WHAT YOU SEE IN HIM.

Alex PEATTIE+TAYLOR

RING RING.

FUMBLE

HELLO... SAY DO YOU KNOW WHAT TIME THIS IS?. WHO IS THIS ANYWAY?

THIS IS THE WOMAN YOU HAVE WRONGED.

OH MY GOD... BRIDGET?

YOU HUSSY. TURNING CLIVE'S HEAD. I KNOW ABOUT YOUR SECRET MEALS IN RESTAURANTS, THE LITTLE PRESENTS YOU'VE GIVEN HIM...

SAY, HOW DID YOU GET THIS NUMBER?

...INCLUDING, I PRESUME, THIS GIMMICKY TELEPHONE WITH VOICE-ACTIVATED DIALLING...

RUTH... RUTH...

DON'T DO IT... BRIDGET...

Alex PEATTIE + TAYLOR

I'M WORRIED ABOUT LEAVING THE BABY UP HERE WHILE THE GUESTS ARE HERE. WHAT HAPPENS IF HE STARTS CRYING?

RELAX, PENNY. THIS BABY ALARM WILL PICK UP THE SOUND OF CRYING AND RELAY IT TO THE RECEIVER IN THE KITCHEN.

YOU SEE, PENNY... WITH MODERN TECHNOLOGY THERE'S NOTHING TO WORRY ABOUT.

IF YOU'RE SURE...

WAAH WAAH

BEEP: HELLO, BABY CHRISTOPHER. I'M AFRAID MUMMY AND DADDY AREN'T ABLE TO RESPOND TO YOUR CALL RIGHT NOW.... IN THE MEANTIME HERE IS A LULLABY...

ANSAPHONE

Alex PEATTIE + TAYLOR

HOME SECURITY

SEEN THIS? A SECURITY TAPE FEATURING SOUNDS OF A DISH-WASHER, VACUUM CLEANER, TV AND HI FI.

IT PLAYS CONTINUOUSLY ON A LOOP. TO ANYONE OUTSIDE A HOUSE IT GIVES AN IMPRESSION OF ACTIVITY WITHIN.

WHAT'S IT FOR? BURGLARS?

YES. IT'S A BIG SELLER, APPARENTLY. CRIME FIGURES HAVE FALLEN DRAMATICALLY.

...AND NOW ON BBC 1. VOOOM... SLOOOSH!

BE FAIR, DARLING. IT'LL IMPRESS THE NEIGHBOURS...

WHY CAN'T YOU GET OFF YOUR BUM AND DO A BURGLARY, YOU LAZY SOD?

Alex
PEATTIE + TAYLOR

Panel 1: Dear Penny and Christopher, Having a marvellous time here in Bangkok.

Panel 2: Business negotiations going well, food excellent, weather superb. Love, Alex.

Panel 3: (silent)

Panel 4: x x x

Panel 5: I DON'T KNOW WHY HE BOTHERS, CHRISTOPHER. WE KNOW HE ALWAYS HAS A SUITE.

Excelsior Hotel, Bangkok

Alex
PEATTIE + TAYLOR

Panel 1: I MUST SAY, I'M BEGINNING TO ENJOY THIS STROLL THROUGH THE FLESHPOTS OF BANGKOK.

WE LOVE YOU CLUB

Panel 2: THERE'S A FEELING OF FREEDOM AND LICENCE HERE... A SENSE THAT THE BURDEN OF WESTERN SEXUAL HANG-UPS NEED NOT APPLY IN THIS MILIEU.

Panel 3: OF COURSE I'M AWARE THAT IT'S ALL AN ILLUSION... THAT DAYLIGHT WOULD OFFER A VERY DIFFERENT PICTURE.

Panel 4: MUCH IS HIDDEN BY THE SEMI-DARKNESS AND THE FLATTERING RED LIGHTS...

YANKEE

Panel 5: YOU'RE NOT STILL BLUSHING, ARE YOU?

BLOW HEAVEN

SHHH. OF COURSE.

Alex PEATTIE + TAYLOR

NO, BRIDGET... CLIVE'S NOT HERE... I HAVEN'T SEEN HIM FOR WEEKS...

THAT'LL BE HER AGAIN, NO DOUBT. THIS IS THE ADVANTAGE OF HAVING A PORTABLE TELEPHONE: PEOPLE CAN'T TELL WHERE YOU ARE.

RING RING.

HELLO BRIDGET... YES, SORRY... I'M STILL STUCK IN THIS MEETING.

RING RING

THIS IS THE ADVANTAGE OF HAVING A PORTABLE TELEPHONE, CLIVE: I CAN FIND OUT EXACTLY WHERE YOU ARE.

BRRR BRRR. RING RING

EEK!

Alex PEATTIE + TAYLOR

SO ALEX RATHER OVER-INDULGED HIMSELF ON THE JAPANESE NOSH?

'FRAID SO.

APPARENTLY ALL THE WINDOWS OF TOKYO RESTAURANTS HAVE THESE MOUTH-WATERING PLASTIC REPLICAS OF THE DISHES ON THE MENU, WITH PRICES MARKED ON THEM, TO ENTICE IN THE CUSTOMERS.

MUST BE TEMPTING FOR THE FOREIGN TRAVELLER.

I SUPPOSE IT'S ALSO MORE DIRECT THAN GIVING LENGTHY DESCRIPTIONS OF THE INGREDIENTS.

WELL, HOW LONG WOULD HE USUALLY TAKE?

...AND THIS IS WHAT I HAD IN THE INN OF A THOUSAND PERFECT BUTTERFLIES...

Alex
PEATTIE + TAYLOR

LOOK, ALEX, THE GOVERNMENT SHOULD BE COMBATING THE FALLING BIRTH-RATE BY INVESTING IN CHILD-CARE SCHEMES.

SURELY THAT'S NOT THE SOLUTION.

BUT THERE'S GOING TO BE AN ENORMOUS SLUMP IN THE POPULATION BY THE MIDDLE OF THE NEXT DECADE. GETTING MOTHERS WITH YOUNG CHILDREN OUT OF THE HOUSE WILL BE CRUCIAL.

IN 4 YEARS THERE WILL BE ⅓ FEWER SIXTEEN-YEAR-OLDS. IMAGINE THE SHORTFALL IN THE LABOUR MARKET <u>THAT'S</u> GOING TO CAUSE.

I SEE WHAT YOU MEAN.

HELLO, MRS GREATBACH? ... YOUR TANYA'S 13 ISN'T SHE? ... GOOD... WE'D LIKE TO BOOK HER TO BABYSIT FOR US DURING GLYNDEBOURNE, 1993...

ICE

Alex
PEATTIE + TAYLOR

IT'LL SOON BE TIME TO LEAVE THE HOTEL AND HEAD OUT ONTO THE STREETS OF NEW YORK, ALEX. GOT YOUR BAG PACKED?

YES.

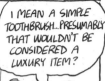

YOU KNOW THAT AT THE FINAL BRIEFING MEETING THE TEAM LEADER GOES THROUGH OUR BAGS AND REMOVES ALL NON-ESSENTIAL ITEMS?

I MEAN A SIMPLE TOOTHBRUSH...PRESUMABLY THAT WOULDN'T BE CONSIDERED A LUXURY ITEM?

NO. I DON'T THINK SO.

RIGHT... GET RID OF THAT AND PUT THE ELECTRIC IN... NO SENSE IN WASTING SPACE.

3 SETS OF GOLD CUFF LINKS? ...A PORTABLE TROUSER PRESS?...

Alex
PEATTIE + TAYLOR

THIS NEW YORK OUTWARD BOUND COURSE: WHAT'S IT ALL ABOUT?

WELL THE BANK AIMS TO TEACH EMPLOYEES A BASIC LESSON IN SURVIVAL.

THESE COURSES ARE DESIGNED TO BRING OUT THE ESSENTIAL VALUE OF EACH TEAM MEMBER...IT'S A CHANCE FOR THEM TO RELATE TO EACH OTHER 'MAN TO MAN'.

OUTSIDE THE OFFICE, STRIPPED OF THEIR SUITS, GOLD WATCHES CREDIT CARDS ETC, THEY GET TO RE-LEARN THE FUNDAMENTALS.

THAT BASICALLY THEY'RE COMPLETE NOBODIES?

EXACTLY. MUSTN'T LET THEM GET COMPLACENT.

Alex
PEATTIE + TAYLOR

BETTER FACE UP TO IT, CLIVE. WE HAVE JUST ENOUGH MONEY FOR STARVATION RATIONS.

WHICH MEANS BASICALLY WE SHALL HAVE TO SUBSIST ON WHAT WE CAN SCAVENGE FROM TRASH CANS.

AFTER ALL, SOME PEOPLE LIVE LIKE THIS ALL THE TIME... GOD KNOWS HOW.

HERE WE ARE... OH GOD...

WHAT?

IT'S YESTERDAY'S.

THIS IS GOING TO BE HELL.

Alex
PEATTIE + TAYLOR

IT'S GROWING DARK AND WE'RE ABOUT TO HIT THE TOUGHEST STREETS IN THE WORLD WITH HARDLY TWO NICKELS TO RUB TOGETHER... I'M NOT LOOKING FORWARD TO THIS...

I'M A LITTLE TREPIDATIOUS MYSELF...

PEOPLE ARE BEGINNING TO STARE AT US... IF WE'RE GOING TO SURVIVE THIS WE HAVE TO TRY TO LOOK MEAN... REAL MEAN.

RIGHT.

RECKON WE CAN PULL IT OFF? IT'S NOT EXACTLY NATURAL FOR EITHER OF US.

WE CAN DO IT.

I SAY... SHALL I HAIL A TAXI YOUR LORDSHIP?

AND FRITTER AWAY MY ANCESTRAL FORTUNE? BOTHER YOU, CHIVERS. BESIDES, THE WALK WILL DO US GOOD...

Alex
PEATTIE + TAYLOR

CHIN UP, CLIVE.

I'M SORRY, ALEX, BUT 5 DAYS LIVING IN NEW YORK FORCES ONE TO CONTEMPLATE THE STARK REALITIES OF LIFE...

IT'S SOMETHING I CONSCIOUSLY AVOIDED COMING TO TERMS WITH WHEN I TRAVELLED ROUND INDIA 6 YEARS AGO... UNLIKE SOME OF MY FRIENDS WHO WENT OUT THERE...

LOOK, CLIVE, SOON YOU'LL BE BACK IN YOUR PROFESSIONAL ENVIRONMENT AND YOU CAN FORGET ALL ABOUT THIS.

IT WILL HAUNT ME FOR EVER.

I CAN'T SEE WHAT YOU'D WANT A BEARD FOR ANYWAY.

I ALWAYS SUSPECTED IT WOULDN'T JOIN UP.

HEY YOU!... YOU'RE A LOUSY BUM.

I'M STILL LEARNING.

Alex
PEATTIE + TAYLOR

WOW! 9 DAYS OF LIVING ROUGH AND NOW A NIGHT IN A BRONX JAIL! IT'S BEEN QUITE AN EXPERIENCE.

FOR THE FIRST TIME IN MY LIFE I'VE BEEN COMPLETELY UNACCOUNTED FOR... 1000s OF MILES FROM HOME, SURVIVING ON MY OWN INITIATIVE... NO ONE FROM THE BANK EVEN KNOWS WHERE I'VE BEEN.

I MUST SAY IT'S GOING TO BE A REAL JOLT RETURNING TO MY NORMAL LIFE AFTER ALL THIS.

YES, IT'LL FEEL PRETTY WEIRD, CLIVE.

I MEAN, NORMALLY FOLLOWING THOSE CIRCUMSTANCES MY EXPENSE CLAIM WOULD BE ASTRONOMICAL.

Memo: From R. Sterling to all directors. Re: Electricity Flotation.

POK POK

In order to ensure the successful outcome of the above, it is important to clarify the objective of economic viability and long-term consumer benefit in the post-privatised industry.

POK POK POK POK POK

However, because the power grid will have to continue to use pressurised water reactors, There exists an exception to This policy.:

POK POK

It is the higher cost of that sector of energy production which must remain nuclear.

DAMN.

It is the higher cost of that sector of energy production which must remain nuclear.

TAP TAP

It is the higher cost of that sector of energy production which must remain unclear.

...AND "PRINT".

POK

Alex PEATTIE + TAYLOR

IT'S AMAZING HOW THINGS CHANGE IN JUST 3 WEEKS... IT'S AS IF EAST GERMANY IS COMPLETELY GOING BACK ON ITS MOST BASIC SOCIALIST PRINCIPLES...

YOU REALLY THINK IT'S SO FUNDAMENTAL?

WELL LOOK WHAT'S ALREADY HAPPENING... TALK OF CLOSER ECONOMIC TIES WITH WESTERN COUNTERPARTS... SHOPPING TRIPS TO CAPITALIST BERLIN... BORDERS OPENING UP TO PRIVATE ENTERPRISE.

I DON'T KNOW HOW YOU'D INTERPRET ALL THAT IN TERMS OF MARX.

BUY INTO THEM FAST, I GUESS.

Alex PEATTIE + TAYLOR

OF COURSE, THINGS HAVE CHANGED AT THE BANK SINCE YOU WORKED THERE, TIBBS. YOU KNOW, WE'VE EVEN DISCONTINUED OUR LEGENDARY IN-HOUSE BREAKFASTS.

REALLY?

WELL, GONE ARE THE DAYS WHEN OUR TRADERS WERE SUPPOSED TO SLEEP FOUR HOURS A NIGHT AND LIVE ON NERVOUS ENERGY AND ADRENALIN.

YOU REMEMBER COMING IN AT 6 AM AND TUCKING INTO A FULL ENGLISH BREAKFAST OF SAUSAGES EGGS AND BACON?

YES I DO

AND BEING SACKED BY YOU STRAIGHT AFTERWARDS.

TIBBS, I TOLD YOU, ANYONE WHO COULD FACE THAT WITHOUT THROWING UP COULDN'T BE GIVING ME 100%...

Alex
PEATTIE + TAYLOR

BUT, ALEX, PEOPLE ARE SAYING THE 90s WILL BE DIFFERENT, THAT THE MATERIALISTIC RAT RACE CAN'T GO ON LIKE THIS.

IN THE 80s EVERYONE WAS BUYING THESE FAST, HIGH-PERFORMANCE CARS - PORSCHES AND BMWs...

BUT WE'VE NOW REACHED A STATE WHERE TRAFFIC IS MOVING AT WALKING PACE THROUGH LONDON. OBVIOUSLY PEOPLE HAVE A DIFFERENT SET OF PRIORITIES.

YES, UPHOLSTERY AND IN-CAR ACCESSORIES.

Alex
PEATTIE + TAYLOR

IT SAYS IN MY BABY BOOK THAT A SMALL BABY IS OFTEN VERY INSECURE ABOUT TAKING A BATH.

YOU HAVE TO WATCH OUT THEY DON'T CATCH A COLD, YOU MEAN?

ACTUALLY IT'S MORE A QUESTION OF THEM NOT LIKING THE FEELING OF BEING EXPOSED.

AT THAT AGE? REALLY?

YES. THEY PREFER TO HAVE THEIR LITTLE BOTTOMS COVERED.

MY WORD!

WELL IN THAT CASE HE'LL BE GLAD TO KNOW I'VE HEDGED HIS ENTIRE STOCK PORTFOLIO WITH TEN YEAR BOND WARRANTS.

Alex
PEATTIE + TAYLOR

NOW, COME WITNESS THE LEGACY OF SELFISHNESS THAT THE 20TH CENTURY HAS HANDED DOWN THE YEARS.

THE POLLUTION CAUSED BY THE MASS PRODUCTION OF PLASTICS AND OTHER NON-BIODEGRADABLE SUBSTANCES WHICH REMAIN ON THE PLANET LONG AFTER THE LIKES OF YOU HAVE ROTTED AWAY TO DUST.

YES, EVEN AS WE PASS INTO THE 25TH CENTURY WE WILL SEE THE EFFECT ON DISTANT GENERATIONS.

ER...

I BELIEVE THESE PRIMITIVE ARTEFACTS WERE KNOWN AS "CREDIT CARDS".

YES. THIS SPECIMEN APPEARS TO HAVE POSSESSED AN UNUSUALLY LARGE NUMBER OF THEM.

ARCHAEOLOGY ROBOT MK16

Alex
PEATTIE + TAYLOR

RING RING

AH... THAT'LL BE ALEX ON HIS CARPHONE. HE TOOK CHRISTOPHER FOR A DRIVE BECAUSE HE WAS CRYING.

MY BABY BOOK SAID THAT THE ROCKING MOTION OF BEING IN A CAR PLUS THE VIBRATION OF THE MOTOR WOULD HELP CALM BABIES WHO ARE RESTLESS.

RING

ALEX! HI! HOW'S THE DRIVE GOING? WHAT'S THE EFFECT ON CHRISTOPHER'S CRYING?

DELIGHTFUL, PENNY, I'M PLEASED TO SAY...

HE'S STILL BAWLING HIS HEAD OFF... EVEN AT 60 MPH THE COMPUTERISED SUSPENSION KEEPS THE CAR PERFECTLY BALANCED... ENGINE NOISE IS AT A WHISPER...

WAAH! WAAH!

Alex
PEATTIE + TAYLOR

HELLO... ER... I'M SURE I'VE SEEN YOU BEFORE SOMEWHERE...

WELL, I HAVE BEEN LUNCHING WITH A LOT OF PEOPLE IN THE CITY BECAUSE OF THE LIKELIHOOD OF LABOUR WINNING THE NEXT ELECTION.

I'M SORRY... ER... WHAT NAME DO YOU GO BY...?

JOHN SMITH.

OH RIGHT! OF COURSE!

NO NAMES, NO PACKDRILL! HEADHUNTER EH? SO WHAT'S THE CHANCES OF GETTING ME A JOB IN EUROPE IF LABOUR FLUKE IN?

Alex
PEATTIE + TAYLOR

SO YOUR HOUSE WAS BADLY DAMAGED BY THE STORM, RUPERT?

THE WIND WAS FEROCIOUS. I'VE NEVER SEEN SUCH DEVASTATION.

OF COURSE THE LOCAL BUILDERS HAVE BEEN INUNDATED WITH WORK BUT LUCKILY I PERSUADED THEM TO START ON MINE FIRST.

YOU SHOULD SEE IT. THERE'S MASONRY ALL OVER THE PLACE.

I SUPPOSE BEING ON THE SQUARE, ONE EXPECTS PREFERENTIAL TREATMENT.

NATURALLY. I AM MASTER OF THE LODGE AFTER ALL.

Alex PEATTIE + TAYLOR

AS A FATHER, ALEX, YOU MUST BE WORRIED BY THE UPHEAVALS TAKING PLACE IN THE BRITISH EDUCATION SYSTEM.

NOT REALLY, CLIVE. ON THE WHOLE I RATHER APPROVE OF THE CHANGES BEING PROPOSED.

BUT, WHATEVER HAPPENS, CHRISTOPHER IS MY SON AND I CAN'T FORSEE HE'LL HAVE ANY PROBLEMS LEAVING SCHOOL WITH THE 3 'A's NECESSARY TO SECURE A PLACE AT ONE OF THE BETTER UNIVERSITIES.

3 GRADE A 'A' LEVEL PASSES?

NO, A TRIPLE 'A' CREDIT RATING WHEN HE APPLIES FOR HIS STUDENT LOAN.

Alex PEATTIE + TAYLOR

WHAT I HATE ABOUT THIS BANK IS THE WAY WE GET TO CHOOSE OUR OFFICE PAINTINGS IN ORDER OF SENIORITY.

WHICH MEANS THAT, AS THE MOST JUNIOR EXECUTIVE, I GET LEFT WITH THE MOST NAFF PAINTING... I'M EMBARRASSED WHEN I HAVE CLIENTS IN HERE WITH THIS AWFUL UGLY THING ON THE WALL.

BUCK UP, SMEDLEY.

YOU SHOULD USE YOUR IMAGINATION. WHAT'S IMPORTANT IS HOW THE PICTURE RELATES TO ITS SURROUNDINGS. TAKE MORE CARE IN CHOOSING YOUR OFFICE FURNISHINGS.

WHAT YOU NEED IS A MISMATCHED DESK AND CHAIRS, CLASHING SCATTER RUGS, A DESK SCULPTURE OF MAGNETISED PAPERCLIPS, MAYBE A FRAMED HOLOGRAM...

THAT WAY THEY'LL ASSUME YOU'RE A SENIOR EXECUTIVE WITH LOUSY TASTE.

Alex
PEATTIE + TAYLOR

...NOW BEFORE THE SHIPPING FORECAST WE HAVE AN URGENT MESSAGE FOR MR ALEX MASTERLEY...

WHAT?

WOULD MR ALEX MASTERLEY, CURRENTLY BELIEVED TO BE ON A MOTORING HOLIDAY IN THE LAKE DISTRICT...

WHAT? IT CAN'T BE ME...

PLEASE CONTACT THE MIDDLESEX HOSPITAL, WHERE HIS GREAT-UNCLE, MR HOWARD CUTHBERTSON, IS DANGEROUSLY ILL...

IT IS YOU! YOUR FAMILY MUST HAVE PUT OUT THE MESSAGE.

I KNOW...OH GOD... THIS IS AWFUL...

THE BASTARDS... THEY KNOW PERFECTLY WELL I'VE GOT A CAR-PHONE.

I REPEAT: THIS IS A NATIONWIDE BULLETIN FOR MR ALEX MASTERLEY...

CRINGE

I WANT TO DIE...

Alex
PEATTIE + TAYLOR

MY GOD, HE LOOKS TERRIBLE, DOCTOR.

I'D BETTER GIVE IT TO YOU STRAIGHT, ALEX.

YOUR GREAT UNCLE HASN'T GOT LONG... IT COULD BE A MATTER OF HOURS...

OH NO.

THIS IS A TOUGH SITUATION... NOT ONE I'VE EVER HAD TO COPE WITH BEFORE. I'M GOING TO HAVE TO LIE TO HIM.

NO ALEX. I THINK IT BETTER IF YOU TOLD HIM THE TRUTH.

WHAT, ADMIT THAT I'VE SET ASIDE THE WHOLE DAY? YOU'RE JOKING. I SHALL TELL HIM I'VE GOT A MEETING AT 2.30.

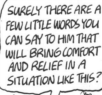

Alex PEATTIE + TAYLOR

WELL, PENNY, I'VE SECURED A LOVELY PLOT UNDER A CHERRY TREE IN THE SOUTH END OF THE CREMATORIUM FOR GREAT UNCLE HOWARD.

HERE'S THE INSCRIPTION I'LL BE PUTTING ON THE PLAQUE.

"IN LOVING MEMORY OF HOWARD CUTHBERTSON. DIED 9TH MARCH 1990 AGED 73 YEARS..."

"...THIS PLAQUE ERECTED BY HIS GREAT NEPHEW ALEX." HOW TOUCHING.

QUITE NORMAL, PENNY.

IT'S PROBABLY A VAIN HOPE BUT WHEN I'M AN OLD MAN IN MY 70s I'D LIKE TO THINK PEOPLE WILL APPRECIATE ME...

...I.E.: REALISE THAT I DIDN'T JUST TAKE OUT THE STANDARD CHEAPSKATE 40-YEAR LEASE...

CEMETERY FREE-

Alex PEATTIE + TAYLOR

MAYBE WE MADE THE WRONG DECISION, ALEX... THOSE WEEKS THAT GREAT UNCLE HOWARD WAS IN HOSPITAL WERE A PRETTY GHASTLY TIME.

LET'S FACE IT... WE KNEW HE WAS GOING TO DIE... I KNOW WE DISCUSSED THE QUESTION OF SWITCHING OFF THE MACHINE.

IT SEEMED WRONG SOMEHOW... BUT MAYBE IT WOULD HAVE BEEN BETTER THAT WAY...

THE NEXT OF KIN HAVE A LOT OF DIFFICULT RESPONSIBILITIES.

EXACTLY. AND I DON'T SEE WHY TRANSCRIBING THE DECEASED'S ANSAFONE MESSAGES SHOULD BE ONE OF THEM.

I'LL GET MY SECRETARY TO DO IT.

...HELLO HOWARD IT'S DAVID MASON AGAIN...

Alex PEATTIE + TAYLOR

CHEER UP, CLIVE... IT'S NOT AS IF WE'RE THE FIRST TOURISTS TO LEAVE LOCH NESS WITH A SENSE OF DISAPPOINTMENT AND FRUSTRATION.

I JUST WISH WE HADN'T BOTHERED TO COME HERE IN THE FIRST PLACE, RUTH. I FEEL SUCH A FOOL.

GETTING UP AT SIX A.M. TO GO FOR A STROLL ALONG THE LOCHSIDE. I SHOULD HAVE KNOWN MY LUCK WOULDN'T CHANGE.

SHOW ME THE PHOTO YOU TOOK OF THE MONSTER AGAIN.

I TORE IT UP. WHAT USE WAS IT? I'M SUPPOSED TO BE AT A CONFERENCE IN BIRMINGHAM.

ISN'T HE A BIT YOUNG FOR THAT?